Tidying Up

The Magic and Secrets of

Decluttering

Your Home and Your Life

Jerry Minchey

www.LifeRV.com

Stony River Media

Minchey, Jerry. Tidying Up—The Magic and Secrets of Decluttering Your Home and Your Life / Jerry Minchey 2016 v.2

ISBN: 978-0-9844968-8-4

1. Nonfiction > Self-Help > Happiness
2. Home Improvement & Design > How-to & Home Improvements

Published by Stony River Media

Knoxville, TN

StonyRiverMedia.com

Dedicated to my mother, Helen Minchey, who showed me many of the tidying concepts that are included in this book. Even when she was in her 90s she would not go to bed until everything was put away and in its place.

I am indebted to Patricia Benton, and Ken Darrow, M.A. (Fiverr.com/MrProofreader), without whose editing, proofing, and formatting this book would not exist.

Contents

Introduction

"There is absolutely no one, apart from yourself, who can prevent you, in the middle of the night, from sneaking down to tidy up the edges of that hunk of cheese at the back of the fridge."

~ Boris Johnson

In this book, I will show you how to tidy up your house once and for all and change your life forever.

Imagine always having a tidy house and never having to tidy up again as long as you live. This book will show you how to make it happen.

Tidying is not just a set of rules about how to discard, sort, organize, and put things in their place. It's also a mindset that makes you a tidy person. Tidying up should be a once-in-a-lifetime event, and it will be if you follow the advice in this book.

For most people tidying up is like losing weight. They've tried to do it many times and nothing works for very long. Regardless of how much effort they put into it, they always end up right back where they started—or worse.

One of the biggest secrets of tidying up is that you don't need so much stuff. Having a lot of stuff actually takes away from your happiness. It's not our fault that we want a lot of stuff. Since as far back as we can remember every TV commercial, newspaper ad, and magazine ad we've seen has tried to convince us that we need to buy more stuff if we want to be happy.

The ads are all trying to convince us to be unhappy with our present life and the things we have. All it takes to be happy, sexy, thin, or wealthy is to buy one more thing— the thing the ad is selling. When we're bombarded with that message over and over for almost every hour we're awake, why wouldn't we believe it?

If you think you don't fall for all of that nonsense, take a look around your house. Why do you have all of that stuff that you don't need? It doesn't make you happy. You have so much stuff that there's no place to put your new stuff, and you can't find the stuff you have now when you need it.

In this book I will show you the simple techniques of tidying up your home and life once and for all. It's easy. You can do it, and the techniques I will describe work wonders. The best part is that your house will stay tidy. You'll never have to go through the tidying up process again.

With the techniques I'll teach you, tidying up is a once-in-a lifetime event.

Here are the three basic secrets for tidying up:

1. Keep only the items that inspire joy in your life. Decide what to keep—not what to discard.

2. Work with one category at a time (clothes, then books, then papers, etc.), and don't try to tidy up one room at a time the way conventional wisdom says to do it.

3. Discard things first, and then organize and store what's left. Do not store things as you go along. Do all of the discarding first.

There are a lot of little things this book will teach you, but these are the three big things that make this technique work where conventional tidying methods have failed.

The first and most important step is to get rid of stuff—and I mean a lot of stuff.

One friend told me, *"As you can see in the picture, I got rid of some of my stuff today, and I'll get rid of more tomorrow."*

When I first started tidying up, that about describes what I did. When you start discarding stuff, it may surprise you how much junk you actually have—maybe not.

Now I live full time in a 34-foot, Class A motorhome, and I have for over three years. When I sit around a campfire and talk to other full-time RVers, one of the topics of conversation that comes up a lot is about how they got rid of so much stuff when they moved from a 3-bedroom house to a 300-square-foot RV.

To do that they all had to get rid of not just a ton of stuff, but in most cases literally several tons of stuff.

I talk to a lot of non-RVers and many of them tell me that they would like to live in an RV, but I hear the same phrase over and over. "I could never do that. I have too much stuff." They say it with the same conviction that they would say one leg is longer than the other one. They act like they were born that way and there is nothing they can do about it.

The interesting thing that always comes out of these conversations with other full-time RVers is that everyone agrees that they have never missed a single thing they got rid of. It's hard to imagine, but I don't recall anyone ever saying they wish they had an item that they had discarded. I know I sure haven't missed any of the junk that I threw away.

When you start discarding things you will be amazed at some of the things you find that you've kept. For example, I put a new spark plug in my lawnmower several years ago. When I took the old one out, it wasn't as bad as I thought it would be, but I put the new one in anyway.

Since the one I took out was in pretty good condition, I kept it. I thought I might need it sometime. I live in a motorhome now. I don't even have a lawnmower anymore, but I found that old spark plug in the bottom of my tool box when I was tidying up.

How many blank VHS tapes do you have that should have been discarded years ago? Speaking of VHS tapes, don't plan on storing important family videos on VHS tapes. Most video experts agree that the life of a video tape is between 8 and 12 years and for best quality, you should convert them to a digital format, and store them on a hard drive within the first five years. Of course, if your tapes are already more than five years old, convert them as soon as possible.

If people can go from a 3-bedroom house down to a 300 square foot RV (or down to a 200 square foot tiny house) and not miss any of the junk they got rid of, you shouldn't have a problem getting rid of enough excess junk to make your house tidy.

In Chapter 2 I'll explain in detail the technique full-time RVers and tiny house owners used to easily get rid of everything they didn't need and didn't want so they could live full time in an RV or tiny house. I call it the RV and tiny house technique of discarding things.

The purpose of this book is to show you how to tidy up once and for all and to convince you that you can make it happen.

Your tidying skills don't get better with age. Is a 50-year old person better at tidying than a 20-year-old? Probably just the opposite.

No place stays tidy for long when people are following the conventional tidying techniques. If you put a new storage building in your backyard, how long do you think it would be before it would be full?

Throwing everything in drawers, under the bed, and back into closets when company is coming makes your house temporarily look tidy, but you know that it's not really tidy. And it won't even look tidy for very long.

When a room is tidy, it will feel so much fresher and brighter, and your mind will feel clearer when you walk into the room. It's amazing. It's hard to describe until you experience it.

Tidying is easy because you're dealing with objects—not people

You're in charge of all of the objects you own and your

decision is final. You don't have to argue with any of the items or try to convince them to see it your way. If you say something goes in the trash or goes to Goodwill, that's where it goes.

Later, when you've finished discarding things and start putting away the things that you've decided to keep that bring you joy, your decision about where to put things is the only one that even gets heard. If you say that an item goes in the top left drawer of your dresser, that's where it goes.

If an item does complain, throw it in the trash. You don't want any stress in your life. After all, how could an item bring you joy if it disagrees with you? The fact that you originally thought the item brought you joy is the only reason it didn't get thrown in the trash to start with.

Most people dread the idea of tidying up their house. They keep putting it off forever. It's a chore they don't look forward to. But when they get into it, they realize that tidying can be fun.

Start with the easy things first and gradually improve your decision-making skills. Before long you will be able to tell as soon as you pick up an item if it stays or gets discarded.

After all, it's your life you're sorting. It either makes you happy or it doesn't. You can quickly tell the items that have served their purpose and outlived their usefulness (and the ones that were never useful in the first place).

Getting rid of useless junk feels so exhilarating.

Note: There are a few places in this book where I have repeated a comment that I made in a previous chapter. I did this because I wanted each section to be complete and stand alone. You don't have to read the book straight through from front to back—although that is recommended.

Bottom line: By the time you finish reading this book, you will be ready to tackle the job of tidying up your home and your life—and you'll be doing it with gusto. You'll be ready because you know you can make it happen.

When you've finished tidying up your house, the phrase, *"Digging through my closet,"* will no longer be in your vocabulary.

Once you've finished tidying your house, you will have this magical feeling. Your house will be in order, your life will be in order, and your world will be in order. And the best part is that it will never revert to chaos again.

Chapter 1

Conventional Wisdom Doesn't Work for Tidying Up

"Be careless in your dress if you must,

but keep a tidy soul."

~ Mark Twain

Most books and articles about tidying up and organizing start with creative ways to come up with more storage space. Implementing all of these new storage and organizing ideas gives the illusion that you have eliminated clutter. The problem with this technique is that, soon, all of this new space is full, and you're back where you started.

To start with, you have to realize that when it comes to tidying up, conventional wisdom is wrong. In fact, most of the tidying techniques you will learn in this book will be showing you how to do just the opposite of what you've been taught about tidying. It shouldn't be hard to give up on those old techniques, you already know they don't work. Forget about techniques like tidying up one room at a time, or doing a little bit each day, or throwing away one thing every day, etc.

Solving a problem by doing the opposite of the way things are normally done is not a new concept. A lot of problems have been solved this way.

For example, Elias Howe is generally accepted as the inventor of the modern day sewing machine. He made his machine work by putting the eye of the needle on the opposite end of the needle from where the eye normally is. In other words, he put the eye of the needle on the same end as the point. That's the whole secret behind how a sewing machine works.

Here's another example of doing the opposite. In the early days of making wood paneling, they were looking for ways to hide the seams where they joined the pieces of wood. The solution they came up with (and it's still being used today) is to do the opposite. Instead of hiding the seams, they make the seams standout. If you look at paneling today, you will usually see a groove painted black where the planks are joined. They don't hide the seams, they exaggerate them.

Since doing the opposite is a proven way to solve a lot of problems, hopefully, it won't come as a big surprise to you that doing the opposite of what most of the "experts" have been teaching about tidying up is the one technique that really works.

It's true. In a lot of cases, conventional wisdom is wrong. That's for sure true when it comes to tiding up.

The five big ways where conventional wisdom is wrong when it comes to tiding up are:

1. Conventional wisdom says to sort by location. — Wrong. Sort by category. (Example, sort clothes, then books, then papers, etc.). Don't sort your bedroom, then your study, etc.

2. Conventional wisdom says the most important part of tidying up is, "Everything has a place and put everything in its place." Wrong. The most important part is to get rid of the stuff that doesn't bring you joy before you even start deciding where to put things.

3. Conventional wisdom says that if you tidy a little each day or discard a few things each day, you'll soon have a tidy house. Wrong again. If you try to tidy up your

house this way, it will never get tidy. If you think about it, I'm sure you've already tried to do this several times, and it didn't work. If that technique had worked you wouldn't be reading this book.

4. The conventional wisdom expounded in most books and articles about getting your house organized and tidy is mostly about clever ways to find more places to store things. Not having enough storage is not the problem. Regardless of how much storage space you have, it will never be enough in the long run. Older houses had one small closet in each bedroom, and it was always crammed full. Now most bedrooms have large walk-in closets, and they're crammed full as well. Having the extra space didn't solve anything.

5. Conventional wisdom says to decide what to get rid of and discard the items that you don't want or don't need. Wrong again. You don't decide what to get rid of, you decide what to keep and then discard everything else.

Remember that there are really only two main goals or tasks that you have to do to tidy up. Decide what to keep and then decide where to put it.

When you check into a hotel room, it's tidy, at least until you start taking things out of your suitcases. Have you ever noticed how clear your mind is when you first settle into a nice hotel room? That's why people sometimes go to a hotel or a cabin for a few days when they have an important project to work on. They find that they're a lot more productive in this uncluttered environment.

Bottom line: Forget everything you think you know about how to have a tidy house. Almost everything you've read or been told about how to tidy up your house is based on conventional wisdom that is totally wrong.

Follow the proven tidying instructions in this book and you will end up with a tidy house that will stay tidy forever more. Tidying is a once-in-a-lifetime event. Do it once and then you'll never have to tidy again. You probably find this hard to believe, but after you read this book, you will understand it, and after you experience it, you will believe it.

Chapter 2:

Discard First

Live your life so you can say, "When I grow up, I want to be like me."

~ Anonymous

Discarding things is the hardest and most important part of your tidying up process. Without fully understanding the topic of discarding, you're doomed to failure. You have to become a discarding expert.

Here is a quote I like about tidying. Maybe it's even more fitting today than when it was written back in the 1800s.

"Have nothing in your house that you do not know to be useful, or believe to be pretty."

~ William Morris

There are two important points to keep in mind when you start your tidying process.

1. Don't think about where to store anything until all of the discarding is completely finished.

2. All of the storage that is done before the discarding is finished is temporary.

Clutter is detrimental to our lives in so many ways. It causes stress, and there's an endless list of problems that stress causes—high blood pressure, lower immunity, heart problems, and the list goes on and on. Getting rid of clutter won't fix all of the problems in your life, but it will sure reduce your level of stress.

Getting rid of clutter will free up brain space too. You might not realize it, but it's hard to think clearly in a cluttered room, and it's really hard to be creative in a cluttered space.

You don't have to live your life being overwhelmed, frustrated, and frazzled by clutter.

Where to Start?

It's important that you sort things in the correct order if you want to be successful at tidying. Clothes first, followed by books, then papers, tools, gadgets, miscellaneous items and finally, photos and sentimental items last.

The hardest thing to get rid of is other people's stuff—gifts, heirlooms, stuff you're stuck with when someone dies. You feel like if you throw their stuff away, it will be like throwing away their memory. There's a lot of guilt when you think about discarding other people's stuff.

Keep in mind that we're not obligated to cherish the same things that our parents, grandparents, and other relatives cherished. We can keep their memories and get rid of their stuff. I know that's easier said than done, but keep in mind that it gets easier when you have some experience discarding things.

So, by all means, sort and tidy sentimental items last. By this time you will be good at knowing what inspires joy and what doesn't. Also, if you sort sentimental items earlier, you'll get bogged down, and the whole process will seem hopeless.

One other point, when you finish discarding everything in all of the categories, your house might look bare and lifeless. Now add some color, flowers, colorful curtains, bedspreads, paintings on the walls, etc. This adds joy, but it doesn't add clutter.

You don't have to add these items all at once, so don't rush to do it. Add a little color at a time until you get your world looking just the way you want it. And, of course, feel free to change things when the mood hits you. You have a blank canvas. You can paint your world to look the way that brings the most joy to your life.

The Secret to Tidying Is to Sort One Category at a Time

I'm sure you've heard the organizational "experts" say things like, "Go through one room at a time or do a little bit each day." I even heard one nut suggest throwing away one item a day. You may have even tried some of these techniques. If you have, you know they are total nonsense. The simple answer is that these techniques don't work.

The only way to tidy up your house is to sort and organize one category at a time—and don't start with sentimental things. That's a recipe for failure. As I've said before, sort sentimental things last.

Start with clothes because they're easy and if you make a mistake, it's no big deal. Once you have more experience deciding what to discard, move on to books, then papers, etc.

When you start on a category, you do <u>not</u> start organizing. The first step is to discard stuff—a lot of stuff. Later, we'll talk about how to organize things, but now your goal is to eliminate a ton of junk.

Criterion—Does It Inspire Joy?

How do you decide what to keep? When you look at all of your stuff, you'll think that some of your stuff is good stuff, some of it is useful stuff, some of it is nice stuff, some of it is expensive stuff, some of it is inherited stuff, some of it is sentimental stuff. But it's still just stuff, and almost all of it is useless stuff that doesn't bring you any joy.

If you were going to walk away from your house and leave everything and you told your neighbor to come by and get what they wanted, and the rest of the stuff was going to Goodwill, how much of it do you think they would take? Some, of course, but not a lot of it because it's just junk (I mean stuff).

When deciding what stuff to keep, some experts have suggested asking yourself questions like:

- Have I worn it in the last six months?

- Do I have anything to go with it?

- Do I have a need for it?

- Does it still work?

- Did I pay a lot for it?

- Would I miss it if it were gone?

- Do I have all of the parts for it?

Forget all of these questions. Don't even ask yourself any of these questions and for sure don't consider the answers to any of them when making your decision about whether to keep something or not. The answers to these questions don't matter.

The only thing that matters is **Does it inspire joy?** This is the most important point in the whole book. But don't stop reading now. You still have to learn how to implement this concept.

What do you do when you can't decide whether something brings you joy or not. The answer is simple. **If in doubt, toss it out.**

You may think that the criterion I've described won't work for all items. For example, you might be thinking that a screwdriver doesn't inspire joy, but you don't want to throw it away. You need a screwdriver every now and then.

Maybe a single screwdriver by itself doesn't inspire much joy, but I dumped all of the tools out of my toolbox and put back in it just the tools that I really liked and enjoyed working with (plus the ones I later found around the house that were supposed to be in the toolbox but had not been put back). When I finished, I had a toolbox that inspired joy big time. Having all of the junk out of my toolbox and having just the tools I liked in there inspired joy.

Rhonda Vincent is known as the queen of bluegrass music. I was at one of her concerts shortly after Christmas one year. She was on stage and between songs someone asked her what her husband got her for Christmas. She said that he got her a toolbox.

Everyone laughed, thinking that's just what a man would do—get her a toolbox instead of something personal. Then she said, "That's what I wanted. I told him I wanted my own toolbox that everyone else would stay out of." So a toolbox really can inspire joy. Maybe not for you, but for me and for Rhonda Vincent it does.

One woman told me that when she is on the fence and picks up something that inspires maybe a little joy, but not much, she asks herself, "Would I be happier without this?" The answer is a simple yes or no, with no emotional complexities.

One woman said that she used the method of picking up things and holding them and then throwing away anything that didn't inspire joy. She said, "So far I've

23

thrown away the bathroom scales, the electric bill, my treadmill, a mirror, the alarm clock, and some Brussels sprouts."

With some items you may want to look at what they do for you instead of looking at the item itself. The item itself may not inspire joy, but what it does for you may inspire joy.

There are things that you need but you don't normally think of them as inspiring joy. Think about when you do need the item, does it make your life happier? That means that you should classify these items as things that bring you joy. A lawnmower may not inspire joy, but what it does for you sure does.

One more thing to consider when deciding whether to discard something or not is its size. I hate to sew on buttons, but a little sewing kit with a couple of needles and pieces of different colors of thread doesn't take up much space, so a sewing kit doesn't have to inspire much joy to justify getting to stay.

On the other hand, I used to have a very large suitcase. When I got it full it was hard to lift and I had to be careful not to go over the airline weight limit. It was useful sometimes, but I never enjoyed using it even though I was happy to have all of my stuff when I arrived somewhere. When I compared the joy it brought me to the amount of space it took up, it was a no-brainer. I got rid of it.

I know I could keep a lot of items inside the suitcase when it wasn't being used—and I did—but it was still always in the way whether it was in the closet or under the bed or even in the attic. Getting rid of that thing brought me a lot of joy. In addition to being happy about getting rid of it, I sold it on eBay and it brought a lot more than I expected. I assume that now it's making someone, somewhere, happy.

Deciding what inspires joy will become easier and you will be able to do it faster with a little practice. As I've said before, start with clothes. Most people have way too many clothes. Most people have clothes they've had for a long time that they've never worn. Clothes take up a lot of space.

The way you decide if an item brings you joy is to pick it up and hold it with both hands (maybe even hold it close to you like you're giving it a hug). Don't try to make your decision about whether an item inspires joy in your life by just looking at it. **You have to hold it.** Note: For some big items (like your treadmill), you don't have to pick it up and hold it, you can just touch it and decide.

If you're having trouble getting started sorting things and you keep picking up items and thinking that you don't know if they inspire joy or not, try this technique to get you started. Take a pile of shirts and pick out the three you like the best. In other words, if you could only keep three of them, which three would it be?

When you're holding any of these three shirts, you will have an idea what inspiring joy feels like. As you go through the pile you can see how the other items make you feel compared to the three items that you know inspire joy.

It gets easier and faster as you go along. You'll soon be able to decide as soon as you pick an item up whether it inspires joy or not.

There will be some items that you think of as just useful and functional (such as a can opener or turkey roasting pan). You may not think of them as inspiring joy, but think about what they do for you. Having a can opener that works properly and is handy when you need it can make you happy. It's the can opener that doesn't work well that can be frustrating. In fact, you should discard any tool or gadget that doesn't work properly. These items are sources of frustration. Just because you need a can opener doesn't mean that you need that one.

Decide What to Keep, Not What to Discard

Here's how you decide what to get rid of. Actually, you

don't decide what to get rid of. You decide what to keep. This is an important point. Essentially, everything must go except what you decide to keep. Nothing gets a free pass. Every item is gone unless you decide that it inspires joy in your life.

As I said before, work with one category at a time. If you have clothes, books, and papers all in your closet, as you take things out, you lay clothes on the bed to be sorted and you stack books and papers over in the corner to be worked on another day. Take everything out of your closet until it looks as clean as it did the day you first looked in there before you moved in.

Don't let your parents see the things you're going to throw away. It's not your duty to cherish the same things they like. Mothers can lay a guilt trip on you in a heartbeat when they see the things you're throwing away.

Declutter Using the RV and Tiny House Technique

If you were going to move from a three-bedroom house into a 300-square-foot RV, or a 200-square-foot tiny house, you would have to do some major decluttering. Your declutteing is probably not going to be this drastic, but I think there are some things that can be learned by looking at how RVers and tiny house owners handle decluttering.

A lot of this book talks about how to decide what to keep, but there is something else you need to deal with. What do you do with the things you're not going to keep. You could just take it all to Goodwill or throw it in the trash, but here are some other options to consider.

Since full-time RVers and tiny house owners have so much stuff to get rid of, most of them used some version of the steps described below to get rid of their stuff. You won't need to be this drastic, but I think you will find some of their techniques for discarding the stuff that they were not going to take with them to be interesting and useful in your tidying endeavor.

They start with the concept that all of their stuff could be classified into one of four categories, A, B, C and D:

Category A: Things that inspire joy in their life. These are the things they are going to keep. So far, so good—unless this category gets to be more stuff than will fit in the tiny house or RV.

Category B: These are the things that can be sold. You can't sell junk and, let's face it, a lot of the stuff you're going to get rid of is just that—junk. But, many of the items being discarded can be sold. You just have to decide if it's worth the effort.

Craigslist is a great way to sell larger items like furniture. If you price the items right and include pictures, they will usually sell within a week. If an item doesn't sell within a week, lower the price by at least a third and list it again. Be sure to list a phone number where you can be reached most of the time.

When someone is ready to buy something, if they can't get you on the phone, they will call another person selling essentially the same type of item you're offering.

For smaller items, you can use eBay. For both Craigslist and eBay, be sure to show several good quality pictures. Pictures make items sell in a hurry.

Category C: These are the things that you put in a garage sale one Saturday and then take what doesn't sell to Goodwill. This way, at the end of the day, everything in this category is gone.

Basically, Category C items are things that you could buy at Goodwill for almost nothing *IF* you ever really needed them. In this category would be tools, clothes, shoes, gadgets, etc.

When you are able to sell some of the items you're discarding and get some money, it makes it easier to part with these items.

Category D: This category is for sentimental things. A few of these things you will keep, but very few. In the next chapter I will go into detail about what to do with sentimental items.

Some people just put everything they're discarding in two

piles. One is trash and one goes to Goodwill or a thrift store. There could be a third pile of things you're going to give to friends or relatives. Whether to go through the process of selling some of your stuff or not will mainly depend on whether it will bring enough to be worth your while.

For people moving into RVs or tiny houses, most of them found it worthwhile to sell some of their discarded stuff since they were getting rid of a lot of things and some valuable things. If you're just tidying up your house, you will be getting rid of a lot of stuff, but whether it's valuable enough for you to make enough money selling it to justify the time and effort required to sell it is a decision for you to make. Sometimes it is and in many cases it's not.

Clutter Is Caused by Having Too Much Stuff—Duh

Of course, everyone knows that, but stop and think about the fact that the average home today has three times more space than the average home did 50 years ago, yet the personal storage business is a $20 billion industry.

We buy things for the same reason we eat—to satisfy a craving.

Even after you have gotten rid of all of the clutter in your house and have an organized and clutter-free house, what are you going to do about all of the stuff that keeps coming into your house—almost on a daily basis?

You buy stuff (when you find a deal that's too good to pass up); parents and grandparents keep giving you or your children stuff (and, of course, you can't get rid of gifts). You have to stop the flow of stuff coming into your home or you'll never have a clutter-free house.

Start by realizing that going shopping is no longer a form of entertainment. If you buy something new, something old has to go out. If you buy a new pair of shoes, you need to discard an old pair of shoes. I know that's easier said than done, but you can't have a clutter-free house if you have a truck backing up to your door every day bringing in a load of stuff. The first step is to realize this fact and then deal with it.

It's Good News If You Find You've Discarded Something You Wish You Still Had

Here's why. You don't have a crystal ball, so you can never know for sure if you'll ever need an item you're considering throwing away, but **if you never find yourself needing something you've discarded, it means that you're not getting rid of nearly enough stuff.**

Another advantage of throwing away a lot of stuff is that you can quickly know if you have an item or not.

Knowing for sure that you don't have an item makes life so much simpler. If you don't have it, you can solve the problem—do without it, buy another one or whatever.

If you don't know for sure if you have the item or not, that could be a bigger problem—you have to keep searching. An even worse problem is when you know for sure that you have it but you just can't find it. It's hard to give up searching for something when you know you have it somewhere. And you feel really bad buying another one when you know that, sooner or later, the one you have will show up.

If you know that you have thrown it away, that's a relief. You can solve the problem—buy another one if really necessary, get by without it or whatever. Either way, it's an easy, stress-free solution. Even if you have to spend money buying something that you think maybe you shouldn't have thrown away, it's not a big problem because it happens so infrequently that you can consider it a small price to pay for the freedom from all of that stuff.

One of the best side benefits of getting rid of stuff is that you will always know what you have and don't have (or you can quickly find out)—and you know where things are.

Back before I did my tidying up, I remember my mother

asking me to connect a DVR that she had bought at a yard sale. It was a simple process of plugging in the cables to connect the DVR to her TV, but since she bought the DVR at a yard sale, she didn't get the cables that came with it. No problem, I remembered that I had a set of cables in my storage unit.

I knew that I had the right cables because I had bought them for a quarter at a yard sale about six months earlier. At that price I couldn't pass them up. I searched through the storage unit for two hours before I gave up and went to Radio Shack and paid $8 to buy the cables I needed. I was 100% sure that I had the cables and I was right. I found them about six months later when I was emptying out my storage unit.

Having something and not being able to find it is frustrating. Also, not knowing for sure if you have something or not is frustrating. You don't know if you should keep looking.

When your house is tidy, you will know right where everything you own is—or you can find it in a heartbeat. Now if I needed cables to connect a DVR to a TV, I can quickly find out if I have the right cables or not because all of my electronic items are in one place—in a box on the top shelf of my closet. It's important to have all things within each category of items stored in the same place. Don't have electronic items stored in three different places.

Being able to say beyond a shadow of a doubt that you don't have something is a liberating feeling. Knowing that you don't have something frees you to make a decision about what you're going to do. It may mean spending money to buy something that you threw away, but the good news is that there's no stress involved. You are free to make a decision, do what needs to be done and then move on.

What's the difference between spending $8 to replace something that you threw away and spending $8 to buy something you didn't throw away but can't find when you need it?

Your job is to get rid of stuff. Err on the side of throwing something away you might later wish you you still had instead of keeping something that you might need sometime. After all, almost everything you own could fit in the category that you might need it sometime.

You don't have to do a perfect job of discarding things. You just need to get the job done. I like the expression, **"Done trumps everything."**

All of our life we've been told, "Always do your best," or, "Give it your best effort." I think it's better to go with the phrase, "If something only halfway needs doing, only halfway do it." Not everything you do needs your best effort. This is another case where conventional wisdom is wrong.

For example, if you're baking cupcakes for a Cub Scout meeting and they crumble some when you're taking them out of the pan, just put more icing on them and serve them. But if you're baking cupcakes for your bridge club and they crumble, maybe you had better start over and bake another batch.

Sorting is something that doesn't need your best effort. You don't have to do a perfect job. You just have to make decisions and move on to the next item.

Bottom line: When discarding things, follow Larry the Cable Guy's motto of "Git-R-Done." Remember, if you don't know if something inspires joy or not—it doesn't. If it did, you would know it.

Chapter 3

The Secrets of Sorting

"Don't own so much clutter that you will be relieved to see your house catch fire."

~ Wendell Berry

Start with the easy things first. Tackle categories in the order I've listed things below, that is clothes, books, papers, etc. I've said this before, but it's worth repeating because it's essential to the success of your tidying endeavor.

And, as I've said before, by all means keep sentimental items and pictures until the very last for two reasons.

First, they are the hardest to make decisions about and by the time you finish sorting the other items, you will be much better at making decisions about whether an item inspires joy or not. The second reason is that it's too easy to get bogged down and spend way too much time in this category.

There are several reasons to start with clothes. First, clothes are taking up a large part of your home, you have way too many, they're the easiest to sort and make decisions about, and a lot of your clothes don't inspire joy. You will have made a big dent in your clutter when you finish sorting and discarding the clothes that don't bring you joy.

Also, working with clothes is a good way to learn how to sort and decide what to keep that brings you joy. After all, if you make a mistake and discard an item of clothing that you later wish you had kept, it's no big deal. It's not like you discarded something that's irreplaceable.

How to Sort Clothes

Now you're ready to start sorting your clothes. The secret is that you pick up each piece of clothing, hold it in your hand and ask yourself if it inspires joy. If it inspires joy, you will know it immediately. If you're not sure, get rid of it.

Start by placing every article of clothing you own on the bed, and scattered around the room on the floor. It's going to take a lot of space to get all of your clothes out at one time. Search the house. Look in every closet, every drawer, and the attic and find every piece of clothing (including everything associated with clothing—belts, underwear, socks, etc.). Don't forget the off-season clothes that you have in storage.

When you've finished, search the house again and find all of the items of clothing that you missed the first time (and, believe me, you will find more clothes the second time you search). How about clothes that are in your car or in the washer or dryer? Don't forget those. Are there any clothes stored in a suitcase or a cedar chest?

Don't even think about sorting or discarding any clothing until you have it all in one pile.

When you finish you will have a pile so big that you can't begin to deal with it, so the next step is to sort your pile of clothes into subcategories. Don't think about whether you're going to keep or discard any item yet. You can decide on your own subcategories, but here are some categories to consider:

- Tops (shirts, blouses, etc.). When you get ready to start sorting, start with these. They're the easiest to make decisions about

- Bottoms (pants, skirts, etc.)

- Hanging clothes (dress shirts, jackets, suits, coats, and some dresses)

- Special event clothes (evening dresses, uniforms, swimsuits, etc.)

- Shoes

- Underwear

- Socks

- Coats

- Sweaters

- Miscellaneous (belts, handbags, scarves, hats, etc.). I don't include jewelry as clothing

Don't save old clothes to wear around the house. What you choose to wear around the house will have a lot to do with your self-image.

I remember two events that changed my thinking about wearing old clothes. As a young engineer I remember one time not long after I was out of school, my boss announced that he wanted everyone in our department to come in on Saturday to work on a project that was running behind schedule. Later in the day, I saw him in the hall and he told me that when working on Saturdays, we didn't have to wear a tie like we did during the week.

He said that people just dressed casually.

I came in with a shirt with a frayed sleeve and some old dress pants. I found out that everyone else was wearing spiffy sports clothes. Their clothes were probably more expensive and newer than those they wore during the week. I quickly learned what was meant by dressing casually for Saturday work. It didn't mean wearing old clothes.

Another example. When I use to paint around the house, I sometimes got paint on my clothes, so when a pair of pants or a shirt became too tattered to wear out of the house, I put it in a bag in the garage to save as painting clothes. When I got ready to move one time and was packing up things, I found that I had three bags of clothes I was saving to wear when I was going to repaint the bedroom. That was a wakeup call.

Bottom line: Don't save old clothes.

Don't store seasonal clothes somewhere out of the way (in the attic, in a storage unit, etc.). Not having seasonal clothes is easy for me to do. Since I live full time in my motorhome, I stay away from extreme temperatures. I stay in Florida in the winter months and in the North Carolina mountains in the summer.

I understand that your wardrobe requirements will be a little more challenging. But look at it this way, regardless of where you live, there are times in the late spring and early summer when it turns cool and you want to wear a jacket or something with long sleeves. Likewise, in the late fall or early winter, there will be times when it turns unusually warm. Both of these conditions happen every year. If your off-season clothes are packed away, you have to make do with clothes that don't fit the weather.

The only reason to store off-season clothes is because you don't have room in your closet for clothes for all seasons. After you finish tidying up that won't be a problem. You will have plenty of room. Having all of your clothes that inspire joy in your life available at your fingertips takes away a lot of stress and brings real joy into your life.

When you start going through your clothes, **remember the two most important rules of sorting.**

1. **You're not deciding what to get rid of—you're deciding what to keep.**

2. **You must handle each piece of clothing. Hold it with both hands.** Don't try to look at an item and decide if it inspires joy.

Most people end up discarding from 50% to 75% of their clothes. You'll almost surely be discarding more clothes than you'll be keeping. That will free up a lot of space in your closet and drawers.

Also, folded clothes take from ¼ to ½ as much space as they do when you hang them. If you stand folded clothes up instead of stacking them, you can see every item at a glance. Don't fold clothes and then stack them. None of them want to be squashed on the bottom and be where they're never seen.

Whole books have been written about how to fold clothes, but to me it's a simple process. There are slight variations based on the item being folded, but, basically, you lay the item flat, run your hand over it to smooth out the wrinkles, and then fold it into a small rectangle or square, smooth the item again and continue folding until it's the size you want.

If you want to become an expert on folding and want to learn details of folding different kinds of items, I recommend Marie Kondo's book *Spark Joy: An Illustrated Master Class on the Art of Organizing and Tidying Up.*

When you put the items in a drawer, stand the items on edge instead of stacking them. That way you can see each item since nothing is stuck on the bottom out of sight. Some flimsy items can be rolled like an eggroll and they will stand up that way.

As you take items out of the drawer some of the items may not remain standing up, but when it's close to laundry time and a lot of items have been taken out of the drawer and items start to fall over, you will be able to see the remaining items with no trouble even if they fall over. The whole idea of not stacking items is so that you can see all of your clothes. Clothes that are out of sight won't get worn.

The solution to a tidy closet. First of all, fold most items and hang very few. Then hang clothes with long ones on the left and short ones on the right. If you look at the bottom of your clothes after you do this, there will be a line going from the bottom left to the top right.

You could just as easily hang the long items on the right and the short ones on the left, but if I said to do it either way that would be one more decision you would have to make—and you have a lot of decisions to make in your tidying process already about which items to keep—so I made this decision for you. Long items on the left. Now you can proceed with your tidying.

In addition to your closet looking neat and tidy when you hang clothes this way, you have the added advantage of now having room on the closet floor on the right side to store things. If you had long and short items mixed all the way across your closet, there wouldn't be much floor space available for you to store things.

It's easy to keep your closet tidy this way. Every time you

start to hang an item back in your closet, just look at its length and see where it fits. That's where you hang it. How much simpler could it be?

How to Sort Books and Magazines

As you did with your clothes sorting process, start by putting all of your books and magazines on the floor. You might think that books are heavy and it takes a lot of work to move all of them. After all, they're easier to see on the shelves, why not just decide which ones to keep by looking at them where they are? The reason not to do it that way is simple. It won't work. So take my word for it and put all of your books on the floor.

You can't decide if a book really inspires joy by looking at it on a shelf. You have to handle it.

Whether you have a lot of books or just a few (nobody has just a few), I recommend that you take them off of the shelves or out of boxes, and put them in different piles on the floor in four or five categories. Depending on the types of books you have, your categories may be different, but here are some categories to consider:

- **Novels**

- **How-to books**

- **Cookbooks, reference books, and manuals**

- **Children's books**

- **Textbooks**

- **Valuable books** – (first editions, collector's items, etc.)
  Most of these are probably not as valuable as you
  think they are. If you think they're valuable, look
  them up on the Internet and see what they're selling
  for. If they're worth a lot, consider selling them. If not,
  stop kidding yourself. I don't know how many times
  I've heard someone say, "This book will be worth
  something one of these days." If they really believed
  that, they should be buying all of the copies they can
  get their hands on now. Since they're not buying more
  copies, it means that they don't really believe it.

Now that you have all of your books on the floor in
categories, just like clothes, make one more trip through
the house and find all of the books that were in unusual
places that you missed the first time.

Now it's time to start sorting books and magazines

Start with magazines

The easiest stack to work on is the stack of magazines.
The easiest solution (and probably the best) is to discard
all magazines—maybe with the exception of this month's
issues that you really are going to read in the next day or
two.

If you haven't read back issues of a magazine, accept the fact that it's not important to you. Magazines are for entertainment and information. Most of the information is available online if you really wanted to know more about a topic, and that includes recipes.

How many magazines do you think you would ever miss if you threw every magazine in your house in the trash? I'm almost sure the answer is zero. If any information in a magazine was of interest to you, you would have read it as soon as it came in if it's a magazine you subscribe to or you would have read it soon after you bought it if you picked it up at the grocery store.

If you discard a magazine that has an article in it that you want to read, all is not lost. After all, don't you have a dentist appointment coming up soon? In their waiting room they will have back issues of magazines going back for years—at least my dentist does. Also, libraries have back issues of most magazines and you can find most magazines online. Be realistic when thinking about keeping any magazine. Does any old magazine really inspire joy? If it does, you have permission to keep it.

Next go to the piles of books

Pick up each book and ask yourself if it inspires joy. Don't start reading it. If you don't know what it's about, I'm sure it doesn't inspire joy.

If you've read the book, the chances of you reading it again are almost zero. If you haven't read it and you've had it for a month or more, you're probably not going to read it. And if you've started reading it and didn't finish it, I don't think you're going to go back and pick up where you left off. After all, if it didn't interest you enough when you were reading it to finish it, why do you think you would want to go back and finish reading it instead of reading a new book?

If any of the books that you have are ones that you think you might want to read (or read again) some time (you probably won't), most books are now available on Amazon as eBooks for $2.99. If you don't have a Kindle eBook reader, you can download an eBook reader app from Amazon for your computer, iPhone or Amazon phone—and it's free.

Printed books are a thing of the past. Some people say they prefer a printed book to an eBook, but most of the people who say that have never spent any (or at least, not much) time reading an eBook.

As my grandmother used to say, *"People are down on what they're not up on."* Try reading eBooks. You'll like them. It grows on you.

Even better than getting books for $2.99, most new books that come out are offered free for a few days when they're first published. Authors see offering their books free for a few days as a way to get reviews and to get people talking about their book.

Also, whatever type of novel you like to read or whatever topic you want to learn more about, there are new books coming out in that genre every day. Spend $2.99 and get you a new eBook. You'll have the latest information or the latest book by your favorite author.

If you read a lot, Amazon has a program where you can pay $9.99 a month and download as many books as you want. If you're buying more than three books a month, this is a great deal. Not all books are available through this program, but most books are.

What all of this means is that you don't have to be too careful when you start discarding books. You could throw away every book and magazine you own and probably never miss them. And if you did one day wish you had one of your discarded books back, you can most likely buy it for $2.99.

When talking about their books, a lot of people use the phrase that they intend to read that book someday or study that subject someday. If you haven't done it by now, you probably never will, but by discarding the book you will soon know how passionate you are about the topic or book. If you don't miss it, getting rid of the book was the right thing to do. You weren't really ever going to read that book anyway. If you find that you do miss it, buy another copy and this time read it immediately. Don't buy it until you're ready to read it though.

I read a lot, but I haven't read a printed book in years (except to proof my own printed books). I publish all of my books in both the eBook and the printed format. I sell a lot more eBooks than printed books, but there are still people who like printed books. To each his own.

When I say that I haven't read a book in years, I do have a few instruction manuals on how to use some computer software programs and apps that I refer to from time to time, but those manuals are online and I usually just log in to Google and get my answer. I guess the reason I have most of the printed books that I have is because I just haven't taken the time to discard them. I just now stopped writing and got up and looked at the printed books I have. There are only six. One of those is the Bible. I'm sure it wouldn't hurt me to read that one again.

I'll get off of my soapbox and get back to how to sort your books. You could just discard all of them, but take the time to go through the procedure of picking up each book and asking yourself if it inspires joy, just like you did with your clothes. Who knows, you may find some that do inspire joy. By all means keep those.

How to Sort Papers

There is nothing more frustrating to most people than all of the accumulated papers in their house. They feel like they are stuck with them. They can't get rid of them. They might need them sooner or later.

When it comes to tidying up, papers can be a big problem, not because they take up so much space (sometimes they can), but because pieces of paper are everywhere. Deciding what to do with each piece of paper can be difficult because they run the gamut from extremely valuable (maybe even irreplaceable) all the way to worse than useless.

The easy answer is that anything that's paper should be thrown away (with the exception of unused paper towels and toilet paper). If you did throw all papers away, you probably wouldn't regret it, but let's be a little careful just in case.

One thing that would help a lot is to stop the flow of papers coming into your house. Change all credit card statements, bank statements, etc. to paperless. It's easy to do, but don't stop your sorting process right now to do that. That's something you can do later.

Some papers may fall into the sentimental category. Trying to decide what to do with these right now can bog you down, so put anything made out of paper that could remotely be considered sentimental in a box and put it in the sentimental pile to be sorted when you get to the point where you're ready to start sorting sentimental items. This includes pictures. because you haven't gotten around to looking at them (or you did look at them and didn't decide what to do.

The main reason that you have so many papers is either that they are stacking up and you put them aside to deal with later, or you classified them as something that you might need sometime.

Old newspapers can accumulate in a hurry. Make it a habit to throw them away every day—even better, change your subscription to the online version. That's a personal choice, but do one or the other.

When you go through your papers, put them in one of four categories (or piles). Even though you may have of a lot of papers, you should be able to sort them in short order.

All papers should go in one of these four piles.

- **Papers that you'll be using in the next few days.** What goes into this category are things like the paperwork to get your car license tag renewed. You can't handle it immediately because you have to get your car inspected first. Your car insurance bill. You don't want to pay it immediately, you're thinking about changing insurance companies and you're waiting for some quotes. The address of the party you're going to this weekend. Invitation to your reunion. You have to decide and reply. In other words, papers in this pile require your attention. Keep them all in one place and take care of them as soon as you can. My goal is to keep this category empty, but I admit that there are usually a few things in this pile. I keep these papers in a basket on my desk—essentially, in my way. That way I can't forget about them.

- **Papers that you need to keep indefinitely.** (Leases, birth certificate, passport, car titles, warranties and receipts showing purchase dates, mortgage paperwork, insurance policies, etc.). You will almost never need any of these papers and they inspire no joy whatsoever (except maybe your passport), but you have to keep them. Put them all in one folder. Don't bother to sort them in the folder in any particular order. If you ever need any of the papers in this folder, just take a minute and look through the folder until you find what you need.

- **Sentimental.** Anything the least bit sentimental goes in a pile to be looked at later. (Pictures, diaries, etc.). Don't spend time looking at these papers now. You can quickly get distracted.

- **Recycle.** If a piece of paper doesn't fit in one of the three previously listed categories, it goes in the recycle bin immediately. Most of your papers should probably end up in this pile.

A lot of things that used to be on paper can now be done on your computer or your smartphone. A lot of people still prefer to have some things on paper. I do to some extent, but I'm going more and more towards being as close to paperless as possible.

Keep in mind that you have the option of scanning a lot of the paper items that you want to keep, and this will eliminate most of your papers.

Here are things that you should consider changing from paper to paperless:

- **Recipes.** You can either scan them or take a picture of them with your cell phone. Instead of tearing recipes out of magazines or copying down your friend's recipe, just shoot a picture of it and email it to yourself. Then file it on your computer in your recipe folder.

- **Bank statements and credit card statements.**

- **Most bills** can be sent to you electronically (and paid electronically). I don't even own a checkbook. I haven't written a check in years.

- **To-do lists.**

- **Seminar notes.**

- **Information for projects you're working on—or planning on working on.**

- **Manuals.** A lot of things don't even come with a printed manual now. You have to download it and if you want a printed copy, you have to print it out yourself. I used to not like this, but I've adjusted. I now like having manuals on my computer.

Bottom line about sorting and storing papers: Papers cause us a lot of grief and make our house look cluttered. At first you might think that there's not much you can do about most of these papers—you need to keep them—but as I've described, you can get rid of all of your papers except for three file folders (and two of those can be out of sight). You don't want to put the papers that need your attention out of sight, but if you get busy and take care of the things that need your attention, this folder (or box) can be out of sight—until something else comes in that needs your attention that is.

How to Sort Kitchen Items

Don't start tidying up the kitchen until after you have finished with tidying clothes, books, and papers. If you do, it's likely that you will get frustrated and give up before your house is tidy.

By tidying up your clothes, books and papers, you will develop the skills necessary to handle the harder decisions of sorting things in the kitchen.

The kitchen is right behind clothes, books, and papers when it comes to opportunities to get rid of stuff. You have two categories of things to sort in the kitchen—food and things (like gadgets, plates, bowls, pots and pans, coffee mugs, silverware, utensils, etc.).

Start with the refrigerator. I'm not going to go into how to clean out the refrigerator. You know how to do this. Just let me tell you that you'll feel happier when it's done.

One big area where you need to sort things in the kitchen is in the pantry. Take everything out. Clean out the shelves while everything is out.

Be sure to follow the "does it inspire joy?" technique every time you pick up an item. Place the items that you are going to keep in different areas of the kitchen table or countertop. You may want to put a card at each spot marked "Top shelf," "second shelf," etc. This is your temporary storage. After every item has been placed in a category or discarded, you can start placing things on the shelf they have been assigned to. Place the things that will be used often in the front and things that will be used only occasionally in the back. Anything that is going to be placed in the back you might want to reconsider and decide for sure whether it inspires joy and you want to keep it.

There are some things that you might think don't inspire joy at first, but maybe they really do. For example, a box of corn starch doesn't seem like it would inspire joy and I don't use it much, but when a recipe calls for it, I'm happy that I have it. At that point it inspires joy for sure.

Of course, discard any item that is out of date or things you know you won't use. Items that you've had for a while and are still good, place in the front and either use them in the next week or discard them. Don't put them in the back of the pantry again.

A lot of people use their countertops for storage. I admit that it's convenient, but I like my countertop to be bare. I don't even have dishwashing soap on my countertop. The only thing that stays on my countertop is my coffee pot. I guess if I ate toast a lot, I would keep the toaster out, but since I don't eat toast very often, I don't keep the toaster out.

Some people like to keep canisters with flour, sugar, etc. on their countertop. That's a personal preference. If you have a large kitchen with lots of counter space where you can keep canisters away from the stove and sink, it might be okay, but I think you will be much happier with a completely empty countertop. It's so much easier to clean. You might think that this is going overboard, but give it a try and I think you will be pleasantly surprised at how tidy your kitchen looks, and how happy you are with your bare countertop.

The next big area of the kitchen to tackle is the gadgets, plates and bowls, pots and pans, coffee mugs, etc. I've never seen a kitchen that didn't have way too many of these items.

The key is to take everything out of the kitchen drawers and cabinets—top and bottom (except the food items that have already been sorted and put back in). While everything is out, clean the cabinets. Then pick up each item and hold it and decide if it inspires joy. You may think it does, but later you could find that you have two or three more just like it (or almost like it). One of them inspires joy, but not all of them.

The items that you decide to keep go in piles on the table that you have marked as "Bottom left cabinet", etc. Pick up each item and decide if it inspires joy. If it does, place it in a pile that goes back in the cabinet or a drawer. When you are finished and before you put things back in the cabinets and drawers, look at each category pile again and decide if you need all of those items. You need a can opener, but do you need all three of them? You'll be surprised at how many duplicate items you have.

How many dishes do you really need? How many pots and pans? If you're not going to use them, I'm sure they can't inspire any joy. You probably didn't realize how many coffee mugs you had or how many different sets of china. Here's where you do another pass when you can look at all of the items in each pile—okay, maybe it's not really a pile, but a section or corner of the table, cabinet or floor.

At this time, I'm sure you will see a lot more items that you don't want to keep. One item inspires joy; the other two or three don't. Decide which one of the items you want and discard the others.

Be ruthless when it comes to getting rid of kitchen items. Just because there is room to put things in the back of the cabinets and you might use them sometime doesn't mean you want to keep all of those things. Keep only what brings you joy. Remember, having empty space to put things in can bring you joy too. For me, not having to work a miracle every time I want to get a pan out of the cabinet or put it back in inspires joy big time. I like cabinets that are not full. When I come back from grocery shopping, I don't want to have to be a magician to get all of my groceries to fit in the pantry.

How to Sort Tools

How you deal with tools will depend on how much joy they bring you (and how much space you have). If you don't care much for tools and only want them for fixing things when absolutely necessary, a small toolbox with your basic tools in it is what will inspire the most joy for you.

On the other hand, if you're into working on your car, or doing woodworking projects, or making jewelry, tools will likely mean a lot to you. The key to being happy with your tools is to have them organized so you easily know what you have and can get to them.

If you have space in your garage, workshop, or basement where you can put a piece of peg-board on the wall, it is an ideal solution if you have a lot of tools. You can see all of your tools, and reach and get any tool you need.

Of course, you will need to go through your tools and pick each one up and hold it and decide if it inspires joy in order to decide to keep it or not. As with all other items, I'm sure you will come across a lot of tools that you will want to discard. You will probably find a lot of duplicates. Let someone else have them who will use them and enjoy them. You and the tools will both be happier this way.

Look at it this way, getting rid of tools that don't inspire joy in your life frees up space on your wall or in your toolbox for more tools that will make you happy. If you like tools, there's always another tool that you would like to have. Put it on your birthday or Christmas list and maybe someone will buy it for you. Since you got rid of a lot of tools that you didn't like, you will now have just the place for that new tool when you get it.

How to Sort Bathroom Items

Sort bathroom items just like you did your kitchenware. One of your goals is to have nothing on the countertop. Most people have toothpaste, deodorant, hairspray, razors, and so many little bottles that there is no room put another item on the countertop. When a bathroom countertop looks like this, you can imagine how often it gets cleaned.

Sort the bathroom items just like you did things in the kitchen. Take everything out of the cabinets and drawers. Put things in categories. Clean the cabinets and drawers. Then pick up each item and see if it inspires joy. I'm sure you will find that you have multiple bottles and tubes of the same basic item, and you will find a lot of items that are way past their expiration date. Getting rid of these items is a no-brainer. Be sure to get rid of expired and unused medications.

Get rid of extra towels and particularly old, ragged towels. This will free up a lot of space in your bathroom or linen closet. How many towels do you need?

How to Sort Gifts

Deciding what to do with gifts is something that gives most people a problem when they start the tidying process. A gift is something that a friend spent time selecting for you, and they spent their money to buy something to make you happy. In some cases they spent many hours actually making the item for you. For example, I had several afghans in a cedar chest that had been there for years. The number of hours it takes to make one of those is more than I can imagine. I never used any of the afghans, but for years I thought I just couldn't throw them away.

As soon as you receive a gift it has served its purpose

When people give you a gift they want to make you happy. It wasn't their intent to lay a guilt trip on you. Look at gifts this way. When you received the gift it made you happy and it served its purpose. If you hold on to it because you would feel guilty if you discarded it, you are defeating the purpose the giver had in mind when they gave it to you.

When you look at gifts this way, it becomes easy to

discard them—maybe all of them. Some of them need to go in the trash (souvenirs, key rings, wedding gifts that you kept longer than you kept your spouse), but a lot of the gifts could be enjoyed by someone else. People in nursing homes love afghans. Where do you think the afghan would rather be—squashed in the bottom of a cedar chest or draped over the shoulders of someone in a nursing home who appreciates it?

If the only reason you've been keeping any item is because it was a gift, discard it in a heartbeat. The day gifts go out the door is a happy day. It's like a big load has been lifted from you.

By the way, gifts to yourself go out the same door. If you have things that you are keeping because, "I bought this when I was in Costa Rica," or "I bought this for myself on my 40 birthday," out it goes. If it doesn't inspire joy now, it has served its usefulness. Get rid of it.

As a general rule, discard all gifts—unless they for sure inspire joy. If you think maybe a certain gift inspires joy, you're kidding yourself and trying to find a way to justify keeping it. Throw it away and get on with tidying up your house. If it's a useful item, give it to Goodwill and it will make someone else happy.

How to Sort Miscellaneous Items

I'm sure you have a million and one items that fit the category of "Not worth keeping, but too good to throw away," or the category of "I might need this one day."

I like to have a little box to put a few small things in that I don't know what to do with right now—things like keys that I don't know what they go to, etc. You can keep a few small items in this box until you're totally finished tidying up your house. If you haven't found what they go to by then, out they go.

Maybe jewelry should have its own category instead of being including under miscellaneous items, but either way, the procedure for sorting it is the same as with all other items. Pick up each piece and ask yourself if it inspires joy. If not, out it goes. You probably have a lot of jewelry items that were gifts. Treat these items like you would any other gift. Don't feel guilty discarding it. The person who gave it to you wanted to make you happy. They didn't want to lay a guilt trip on you. The item served its purpose when you received it. You're not obligated to keep it forever.

How to Sort Furniture

When you think about discarding things, you were probably not thinking about furniture, but most likely there are several pieces of furniture in your house that don't inspire joy. Get rid of these items in a hurry. If the main purpose of a piece of furniture is for storing things, seriously consider discarding it.

You will need a few places to store socks, underwear, etc., but more than likely you have more pieces of furniture for storing things than you really need. Believe me, regardless of how much storage space you have, it will soon fill up. Having extra storage space is detrimental to having a tidy house.

Also, couches and chairs that don't inspire joy should be discarded. Even if you can't afford to buy new furniture, having a house without a lot of furniture in it would probably bring you more joy than having furniture that you don't like. In my opinion, most houses have way too much furniture and excess furniture makes houses look cluttered.

Most real estate agents will tell you when you're getting ready to put a house on the market that you should get rid of a lot of the furniture (even if you have to put it in storage). It's a known fact that houses look roomier and sell quicker when they're not cluttered—and excess furniture is clutter to prospective buyers.

If you want your house to look uncluttered to prospective buyers, why wouldn't you want it to look uncluttered to you?

How to Sort Sentimental Items (including Pictures)

Sorting sentimental items and pictures was put off until last for two main reasons.

First, since sentimental items are the hardest to make decisions about, it would be a disaster if you started trying to sort these items when you first started tidying and didn't have any experience deciding what inspires joy in your life and what doesn't. But now that you're more experienced, you can make decisions about joy faster and with less stress.

The second reason to sort sentimental items and pictures last is that it's easy to get bogged down and spend way too much time sorting these things. You know how to do it now. You pick up each item, look at it, hold it next to you if you need to, and then you decide. You don't do any second-guessing. Go with your first instincts. Either it inspires joy or it doesn't. Make your decision and move on to the next item.

The simple answer about how to sort and store sentimental items is not to do it. Give the items to other family members (but not family members in your own house) and let them keep them. Clutter up their house. Of course, that probably won't work for everything. You probably have some sentimental items that inspire joy. Those are the items you keep and find a place for. Don't keep something because you would feel guilty if you got rid of it. Don't let guilt guide you. Only keep things that inspire joy.

Pictures are a special kind of sentimental item

The easy thing to do with pictures is to go through them quickly and decide if you have the least bit of interest in keeping them. Put every picture that you think you might want to keep in a box labeled "To-be-scanned" and put all of the others in the "Not-to-be-scanned" box.

This is one case where you don't have to be ruthless in discarding things because you're basically going to discard all of the pictures later anyway after you digitally scan them. The only reason to go through the pictures in the first place is to save you the cost or trouble of scanning pictures that you have absolutely no interest in.

After you scan the pictures you can store the files on a hard drive, thumb drive, or in your Cloud storage and have them. If you don't want to do the scanning or don't know how, there are companies that will do this service for you reasonably inexpensively.

Before you scan the pictures be sure to take the time to write the names of the people who are in the pictures on the edge (or on a sticker that you put below the picture) and write the date and place the picture was taken if you know. Years from now, when you or other family members are looking at the pictures, it would be nice to know who that is standing beside Uncle Bill.

One other thing that I suggest that you do is, when you're finished scanning the pictures, take both boxes of pictures and ask other people in your family (who do not live in your house) if they want the two boxes of pictures. Don't let them pick through them. Tell them to take both boxes and then give any pictures they don't want to anyone else in the family who wants them.

This process accomplishes two things. First, you have the pictures you want stored forever in a digital format. Second, you don't have to feel guilty. You didn't actually throw any of the pictures away. Someone else in the family may have eventually thrown some of the pictures in the trash, but you didn't.

Some people like to sort through printed pictures and select certain ones and put them in an album—not me. If you want to create a picture album, there are software programs that will take digital copies of your photos and arrange them in any order that you like. You can add titles, subtitles, and descriptions and make impressive photo albums. Just don't get sidetracked from your tidying project by trying to do that now. Playing with pictures can eat up a lot of time. That's a project for another time after all of the tidying is finished.

Bottom line: This chapter covers the nuts and bolts of the tidying process. When you complete the chores described in this chapter, the hard part (mentally, physically, and emotionally) is done. You may want to go back and read sections of this chapter again as you go through your sorting process. The important thing is to get it done.

When your whole bedroom is covered with clothes and you can't even find room to walk, it's tempting to give up, but hang in there. You'll make it. Remember you always have the option of just picking out the few things you like and giving everything else to Goodwill or throwing it in the trash. That's basically what you're doing, just in a more systematic way.

Chapter 4:

A Special Place for Every Item You Own

"Out of clutter, find simplicity."

~ Albert Einstein

After you've done all of the discarding, then and only then are you ready to start storing things. All of the storing you've done up until this point is purely temporary storage. Discarding items can take a long time, maybe several days, but putting everything in its place can usually be done in one day—two at the most.

Get Rid of Furniture Used for Storage

Believe it or not, when you have reduced your stuff down to only the things that inspire joy, you will probably realize that you can store the remaining items in the built-in storage that's part of your house. You don't need furniture whose sole purpose is to provide a place to store things—bookcases, dressers, chest of drawers, etc.

Maybe if you have a piece of furniture that's a family heirloom (and it inspires joy), you could consider keeping it, but make sure it really does inspire joy. Of course, if you don't have any built-in drawers, you may need to keep one or more dressers or chests of some kind.

When you start deciding where to store things, start with the plan that furniture used just for storage will no longer be needed in your house. How uncluttered would your house look if all of the furniture that has been used just for storage was gone? Wouldn't that be nice?

Start your storage process with the idea that you're not going to make use of any storage furniture.

Start by storing big items first—space heaters, fans, suitcases, etc. Put them in the back of your closet. Of course, you may find that most of the year either your fan or your space heater will be out and being used.

Designate One Place for Each Type of Item

A few items may go in two places. For example, you will probably hang some shirts and dresses and fold some, but for most items, put all of one type of item in just one place.

The first step is to decide where to store different categories of things. Below is the broad general list of the categories I use to sort my stuff. I tweak it as I go along because some things can fit into more than one category.

You can individualize your storage plan to fit what makes you happy. For example, I store a Phillips screwdriver and a flat-blade screwdriver in the drawer with my silverware and kitchen utensils rather than in my toolbox, which would be the more logical place. I do this because I use them a lot and it's more convenient. Basically, I do it this way because it makes me happy.

Where and how you choose to store things is a personal matter. The important thing is that everything must have a place. You get to make the decisions. Here are the categories I sort things into, and I have a place for each category.

- **Clothes** – I store all of my clothes in one of two clothes closets, and in one of three drawers. My closets have room for hanging clothes and there are shelves in the closets. I have half of one closet that's empty. I like it this way.

- **Fabric items** – Towels, sheets, etc. I store these in a linen closet.

- **Books** – I store these in one small built-in cabinet, which looks like a bookshelf except that it has a door. How you store your books depends on how many books you have and on your decorating preference. I have cut my printed books down to about half a dozen. Almost all of the books I buy now are eBooks and I read them on my Kindle Fire reader, or on my cell phone when I'm not home and don't have my Kindle with me.

- **Papers** – I have eliminated most papers by scanning them, but the few notebooks, index cards, income tax records, business records, maps, etc., that I have, I store in hanging folders in a box that acts like a filing cabinet. I have one small drawer that I use when I want to temporarily put papers away that I'm working on. For example, when I'm proofing a printed copy of a book draft, I can catch some typos and errors better when looking at a printed copy. When I'm finished, I discard the draft copy, but the little drawer is a handy place to keep it for a few days while I'm working on it.

- **Electrical appliances** – I treat these differently from electronic items. The mixer, vacuum cleaner, printer, electric polisher for the car and RV all get stored where they're normally used rather than having them all in one place.

- **Electronics and cameras** – Of course, my computer stays out on my desk, but most other electronic items, chargers, cables, etc., go in a designated electronics drawer.

- **Bathroom items** – Obviously these items go in the bathroom, some in the cabinets and some under the sink if they're not used often. Some people like to have a lot of commonly used items (toothpaste, deodorant, etc.) out on the countertop. That's convenient and functional, but to me the bathroom never looks tidy if the countertop is cluttered—even if it's organized clutter. To each his own on this. I don't have anything on my bathroom countertop.

- **Kitchen items and food stuff** – This is easy. There's lots of storage space in the kitchen. I put the items that are used the most in the convenient places and the infrequently used items on the higher shelves or at the back of the kitchen cabinets. As far as having frequently used items on the countertops, it's a handy and functional way to store things, and a lot of people do it that way; I like to see the countertops clean, so my coffee pot is the only thing that gets to be out on the countertop.

- **Cleaning supplies** – Most of these items go in the cabinet under the kitchen sink. Some are under the bathroom sink.

- **Tools, gadgets, and miscellaneous items** – go in the basement. Yes, a motorhome has a basement just like in a real house; it's a big area under all of the living area. There are five doors on each side to get to this area, so it's a handy storage space. The problem (like most basements) is that it's almost too handy. It's easy to just stick things in the basement (or garage if you have one) and decide what to do with them later. In other words, it can quickly fill up with clutter if you're not careful.

- **Extra Consumable supplies** – Some people like to buy consumable supplies in bulk (packages of eight rolls of paper towels, etc.) to get a better price and to make sure they don't run out. Having an extra bottle of laundry detergent, and extra consumable supplies in general, inspires joy in some people and for other people the amount of space they take up is a source of frustration. It's a personal decision. There's no right or wrong way to do it. Just decide which way inspires the most joy in your life and go for it, but if you choose to have extra supplies of consumables, make sure you designate a place for these extra supplies. My brother stores his extra consumables on top of the standup freezer, which is out in the garage. It's a convenient, handy, and out of the way place. I like to split the difference and keep one extra of about every item that I consume, but I don't buy bulk quantities of any item. I do keep more than one extra roll of paper towels and toilet paper.

- **Hanging clothes** – If you have plenty of closet space for hanging clothes (compared to the amount of clothes you want to hang), then hanging clothes is a good solution for storing a lot of clothes. But if hanging space is at a premium, hang just bulky items such as coats, jackets, suits, and items that wrinkle easily, such as men's dress shirts, and some dresses. Fold the other clothes. Fold clothes and they'll take up about half as much space as they do if you hang them.

- **Hobby items** – Whether your hobby is painting, making jewelry, playing golf, photography, scrap-booking, or something else, it's probably something that inspires joy in your life. You're bound to have some unique items that go with your hobby. By all means, have a special place to store these things. Of course, look at each item you store in this category and give it the "Does it inspire joy?" test. There's bound to be some clutter that you will want to get rid of. That way you can enjoy your hobby a lot more when your toys (I mean tools and necessary items) are sorted and readily available—and all of the junk is gone.

This doesn't describe all of the subcategories that you could have. You can start with more or fewer categories than those I've described and add more as you need them to fit your individual needs.

After discarding all of the clutter and the things that don't inspire joy in your life (plus the furniture you've been using to store all of that stuff), you will likely find that you have a lot more space than you thought you had. Wouldn't that be nice? Having plenty of space for things makes storing them so much easier.

The Hammer Doesn't Have a Place

When I was a little boy my grandfather was at our house for a visit one time. He was working on fixing something and he asked me where the hammer was. I told him I would go find it for him. He wanted to know why the hammer wasn't in its place. I told him that the hammer didn't have a place.

It was most likely wherever my brother or I used it last. Maybe it was in the basement, or in the barn or in our tree house. He could maybe understand that the hammer wasn't put back in its place, but to him the concept of the hammer not having a place was incomprehensible. He couldn't imagine such a thing.

Maybe the hammer had a place. If it did, my brother and I didn't know where it was.

Now in my house the hammer has a place. My grandfather would be proud of me.

Everything should have a place. When I was a kid everything that didn't have a place (except the hammer) was put in the corner drawer in the kitchen. If you couldn't find something, it was probably in the corner drawer in the kitchen.

My mother said that when she was growing up they had a big, wooden box that was behind the wood-burning kitchen stove. It was called a "catch-all." Anything that didn't have a place could usually be found in the catch-all.

Maybe you need to have a catch-all. After all, things that are put in the catch-all are still considered to be in their place.

Make Use of Little Boxes

I like to use the lids to boxes as little boxes. I put these in drawers and then I can take the whole little box out and easily see what's there. I like little boxes in drawers better than dividers. It's easy to look at the items and discard things later when the box starts to get too full. The lids of shoeboxes (or other similar box lids) work great with this technique.

One of the best uses of a little box is that I use a small, empty facial tissue box (not the standard size, but one that's about four inches square). I put plastic grocery bags in it. I can pull them out one at a time just like I would facial tissue. It holds a lot of little plastic bags, but when I notice that it's getting about empty, the next time I go to the grocery store, instead of taking my cloth reusable bags, I have groceries put in the plastic bags and then after I put up my groceries I refill my little box. The box and the system work great. And, best of all, it's tidy.

Stand Things on End

Store items standing vertically (at attention) and you can see them better. Of course, don't leave them that way. Before you close the drawer, give them the, "At ease," command. They will still be vertical, but then they can relax.

Bottom line: If everything doesn't have a place, there's no way for everything to be in its place. And when items are not in their place, your house is not tidy. It will quickly go back to being cluttered, so, by all means, make sure you have a place for everything. If you don't, your tidying up process will have been a waste of time.

Chapter 5

What to Do about Other Family Members Not Being Tidy

"No person who can read is ever successful at cleaning out the attic."

~ Ann Landers

You might be saying "I could tidy things up if I lived by myself, but with this crew it's hopeless."

Don't try to tidy up the whole world. Not even your whole household. Tidy up just your world, just the parts of your house that you're in charge of—your bedroom, the kitchen, your study, laundry room, garage, workshop, or whatever.

When Your World Is Tidy, You're More Tolerant of Untidiness in Others

Once you have the parts of the house you're in charge of (your bedroom, study, kitchen, workshop/garage, etc.) all tidy, you will likely find that you can tolerate a much higher level of untidiness when it comes to other members of your household.

Don't complain and criticize. And don't let it get to you. Your happiness doesn't depend on whether other people's rooms and areas are tidy. Your happiness comes from the part of your world that you're in control of being tidy.

Concentrate on how happy and content you are with your tidy world and let the untidiness of others run off of you like water off of a duck's back.

But maybe there's hope after all. Try the following techniques to get other members of your household to be tidier.

Small Children, Teenagers, and Your Spouse

When it comes to getting your house tidy, accept the fact

that you have almost complete control over yourself (and your stuff), a lot of control over small children, a little control over teenagers, and not much control over your spouse.

Knowing these limits, here are some ways you can accomplish some tidying in each category. Start by not expecting the same level of tidiness that you have achieved. It's not going to happen. Be thankful for small improvements.

Let's start with small children.

By the way, when I say small children here, I'm talking about kids who are old enough to have strong opinions about what they like and don't like. For toddlers, keeping their room tidy is totally your job and you get to make all of the decisions just as though you were decluttering your own space.

The first step is to stop buying them so much stuff. There's no limit to their wants. (Maybe we can say the same thing about ourselves.) Buying them more stuff only gives them joy for a very short period of time.

The first step is to get rid of all of their clothes that don't fit or any clothes that they don't like to wear.

Kids like to play games. You'll likely have some success getting them to play the "decluttering game." Introduce them to the concept of taking all of the items in one category and deciding which things inspire joy and then discarding the others.

First, start with clothes. Next, move on to toys. If the pile of toys is too big, break it into sub-groups. Maybe start with games.

One thing to keep in mind when sorting toys and games is whether all the pieces and parts are there. Maybe a toy or game used to inspire joy, but if some of the pieces or parts are missing, it probably doesn't inspire much (if any) joy. Don't keep a toy or game just because it used to be fun.

Keep these sorting game times short. Remember that kids have short attention spans. Play the game for a short time and then come back and play this game with them again the next day. It won't take long until you will have their room as tidy as yours—well, maybe not that tidy, but at least you can hope.

Next, let's deal with teenagers. Teenagers are like "terrible twos" only eight times worse. You can introduce them to the concept of "Sorting things by category" and the concept of "Does this inspire joy?" It will probably work for getting rid of some of the clothes they've outgrown and clothes that they don't like, but they probably won't discard as many clothes as you would like. Be thankful for small miracles.

Next, try to encourage them to do the same thing with their books, CDs, DVDs, and games, and then papers. Some teenagers actually get into the decluttering thing and some just have no interest in it. Give it a try. You don't have anything to lose.

Your spouse or significant other. Don't ruin your relationship over this. Any progress they make in this area will be because they want to or because they want to make you happy—not because you made them do it, so don't nag. Show appreciation for even slight accomplishments. Explain the "One category at a time" and the "Does it inspire joy?" techniques of sorting and decluttering. Offer to help, but don't dominate. If your opinion is asked for, give it, but don't overdo it. It's not your stuff that's being discarded. You can't decide what inspires joy for someone else. Don't try.

If they ask for your opinion by saying something like, "Does this shirt look good on me?" or, "Should I keep these shoes?" encourage them to discard the item. First of all, I'm sure it doesn't inspire much (if any) joy for them or they wouldn't be asking your opinion.

Don't have high expectations of getting other members of your household to really get into tidying and then you won't be disappointed. Just be thankful for any improvement you see.

When Others See How Tidy and Happy You Are, Maybe They Will Tidy Up Some Too

Getting other family members to tidy up "some" is probably the best you can hope for in most cases. When other family members see how tidy you have made your areas and how happy you are, it may rub off on them and they'll start tidying up—maybe not to the level you did, but you might see them make some amazing improvements. Be thankful for any improvement in their tidying habits.

The situation may not be as hopeless as you think.

One thing to keep in mind about how much other people's lack of tidiness bothers you (or downright irritates you) is that it, may have a lot to do with how you feel about that person. A good example is that if someone you like and admire is smoking nearby, it may bother you slightly, but if someone you strongly dislike is smoking around you, it is unbearable and drives you up the wall. The same goes for tidying. How you feel about someone's untidiness has a lot to do with how you feel about that person in general. I'll get into that more in chapter 7.

What about grandkids? That's one category that we didn't talk about. If you see them a few times a year, don't worry about trying to get them to be tidy, but if you keep them every other weekend and particularly if they keep stuff at your house, that's a different story.

Basically, treat them like kids or teenagers (depending on which category they fit into). Like kids, sometimes you will have success and sometimes not. Don't get stressed out about it. Be happy with any success you are able to achieve.

Bottom line: Other family members will probably do some tidying up, and when your world is tidy and you are happy with yourself, the fact that other people around you are not as tidy as you are will not bother you nearly as much as it did before. In fact, it may not bother you at all. In other words, life is good.

Chapter 6:

The Secrets of Staying Tidy

"Believe you can and you're halfway there."

~ Theodore Roosevelt

When people start thinking about tidying up their home, one thought that goes through their mind is, Yea, I might be able to do that, but this place would be a mess again in no time. They're right. It would be except for two things:

1. After tidying up you won't have so much stuff. There will be plenty of room for everything you own.

2. Everything you do have will have a place. And you will

know where that place is. You won't have to try to find a place to put something when you pick it up.

It's hard to tidy up if you pick something up and don't know what to do with it, but when everything has a place (even the hammer) and you know where that place is, it's easy to go put it in its place.

It won't take long to get into the habit of washing dishes after each meal (or putting them in the dishwasher). And if you've been snacking while you're watching television, it's easy to just want to get up and go to bed and clean up everything in the morning, but it will only take a few minutes to at least put the dishes in the sink, so do it.

Take care of tidying up as you go through the day as much as you can—things like sorting today's mail, throwing away yesterday's newspaper, discarding a magazine that you have finished reading, etc.

By the way, when you sort the mail, if there is something that requires action on your part, make sure that it's put in your "To-do" or "Needs-my-attention" box on your desk. Don't leave it lying somewhere in limbo.

There's a difference between your house being tidy and being clean. There will be times when your house will need to be vacuumed, or dusted, and maybe the dirty clothes basket is full, and there are clothes in the dryer that need to be folded. All of these things are part of daily life. These situations are normal. They don't mean that your house is not tidy.

Unless you live by yourself, you will have to deal with the problem of other family members leaving things lying around and cluttering the place up. One woman told me the solution she was considering was to get her 9mm pistol out and shoot anybody who cluttered up the house. She said that she might lose one or two family members that way, but the others would soon get the message.

I suggested that she just barely miss them on the first shot and see if that would get the message across that she was not going to put up with anyone cluttering up her tidy house. The last time I was in her house it was still tidy, so I guess she found some way to get the message across. I didn't count heads to see if anybody was missing.

Seriously, I know it's frustrating to have to pick up other people's clutter. I'm sure your situation is not totally hopeless. You can get the other family members to more or less pick up their mess. Then just bite the bullet and pick up what they don't get, and in less than a minute a day you can pick up everything. Okay, I understand; with your family it may take you 10 minutes a day to pick up everything. Spend the 10 minutes and you will have a clutter-free house.

Even when my mother was in her 90s she wouldn't go to

bed until everything was picked up. She would always say, "It will only take a minute." And she was right—literally. In 60 seconds you can pick up a lot of stuff and put it where it belongs.

Believe it or not, you will sleep better knowing that your house is tidy. At least I do.

One thing to keep in mind is that, after you discard all of the things that don't bring you joy, you will have plenty of space for things, but nature doesn't tolerate a vacuum. So in no time, all of that extra space will fill up with junk (I mean, useful stuff). Whatever you call it, don't let all of your extra space evaporate.

I like to have unused space to temporarily store projects I'm working on. If I start to fix an antique clock or repair a fishing reel and I don't get finished repairing it (projects always take longer than you expect), I like to have a place to put everything out of the way so I can come back and finish the project the next day.

The problem is that tomorrow I may forget about yesterday's project and start another project and then two weeks later that project is still sitting there taking up that space. You can see how it won't take long until all of the extra space is used up.

You will still have a tidy house (until things start spilling over), but don't let unfinished projects take over all of your extra space.

Earlier this week, I was working on a computer keyboard and, as usual, I didn't get it fixed. When I got ready to go to bed it was still spread out on the kitchen table. It would have been easy to leave it there so I could work on it the next day, but since I had an empty shelf in the closet I carefully put all of the parts on that shelf and had a clean kitchen table for breakfast the next morning.

The next day, I decided to just order a new keyboard through Amazon and with Amazon Prime I had it in two days. Problem solved. In the old days, I would find a place to keep all of the parts from that old keyboard because, who knows, I might need some of those parts to fix the new keyboard sometime if it went bad.

That was my old way of thinking. The next time I saw that disassembled keyboard in the closet, I immediately picked all of the parts up and put them in the trash. Now I have my empty space back. Yes, one of these days I might need one of the rubber feet off of that old keyboard that I threw away. If I do, I'll just deal with it, it won't be the end of the world, but my guess is that the need for any of the parts from that keyboard will never arise. These are just examples of what happens in everyday life and how things seem to work against keeping your house tidy. Be diligent and you will win.

Three tiny tasks that will help you maintain a tidy house.

1. **Make your bed every morning.** Your bedroom can't look tidy if your bed is not made. I can make my bed in less than 30 seconds. It doesn't look like a bed in a five-star hotel and there's no chocolate mint on the pillow, but it's not a mess. Use hassle-free bedding that's easy to straighten and it will be easy.

2. **Don't let dirty dishes accumulate.** Put all dirty dishes in the dishwasher or handwash them and put them up immediately after each meal. No kitchen can look tidy with dirty (or even clean) dishes out. Take care of dishes immediately after snacks too. Don't go to bed and leave dirty dishes (or empty cookie bags) anywhere in the house.

3. **Don't leave anything on the kitchen or dining room table.** It's easy to let items pile up on tables. If junk mail or school books are on the table, other stuff will quickly start showing up there too. Then your tidy house will no longer look tidy.

Bottom line: If you follow my mother's example and never go to bed until everything is picked up and put in its place, your house will always be tidy. What could be simpler than that? How much time could that take? Most of the time your nightly tidying up can be done in less than a minute once you get the hang of it.

Where tidying up becomes time consuming is when you pick up something and don't know what to do with it. That's not the case in your house anymore because everything has a place.

Chapter 7

Get Rid of Everything That Doesn't Make You Happy . . . Even if it's a Spouse

"Any fool can criticize, condemn, and complain—and most fools do."

~ Benjamin Franklin

You can't be totally happy if your life is not tidy. But if you dislike almost everything about your spouse or significant other, you're probably not going to be happy regardless of how tidy your house is.

But before you throw your spouse out with all of the other junk in your life, give your new tidy world a little time. Here are some things to consider:

- When your house is tidy and you like yourself, your spouse might start liking you more too (and showing it).

- When your house is tidy, you may find that it wasn't your spouse that was bothering you as much as you thought.

- The whole world (and the people in it) takes on a different look when your house is tidy and you feel in control.

- I'm not saying that a tidy house will fix all relationships, but it might do a lot more than you thought possible. It won't hurt to give it a little time.

But if all else fails, you now know how to get rid of things and how to decide what you want to keep.

Use the criterion "Does this 'thing' inspire joy in my life?" If not, you know what to do.

When your house is tidy, you'll have a lot more confidence. Your inferiority complex will be gone. After all, it should be gone. You're not inferior. Just the opposite. You've accomplished what most people only dream about—having a tidy house.

I've heard the opinion expressed that some people have a justifiable inferiority complex. Maybe some people do, but not you. At least not now.

Having confidence in yourself will work wonders in your life. Of course, I guess you can overdo it. I remember when I was taking flying lessons to get my instrument rating to go with my private pilot's license my flight instructor told me one time that I had more confidence than skill. That's not such a good thing when you're coming in for a landing on a dark, foggy night with minimum visibility. I now have over 2,000 hours of flying time, so hopefully I have gained the skill to go with the confidence I had back then.

Back to tidying up and relationships.

You have more space in your house when it's tidy. You also have more space in your mind. You can use that space to sort through your feelings. One thing you will notice when your house is tidy and in order is that you no longer feel anxious and uptight. Having that relaxed feeling makes it a lot easier to decide what's really important in your life, what you want to do with your life, and who you want to spend your life with.

Take some time to live life in your tidy house. You will see some changes in how you see yourself and the world.

You will find that you're a lot more tolerant of people and things that used to drive you up the wall—including your spouse.

On the other hand, you will find that you're a lot clearer about what you like and dislike and about what you want and don't want. One thing that I think you will experience is that your relationship with your significant other will change—maybe only slightly and maybe more than slightly. And things may improve or go to hell in a hand basket, but they will change. In most cases, I think relationships will get better, but tidying up doesn't guarantee this.

One thing is for sure. Little things that used to bother you about your spouse won't irritate you nearly as much when you're not dissatisfied with your life and the world in general like you were when your house wasn't tidy. And when your attitude about yourself and the world in general changes, you will be a much more likeable, loveable, and forgiving person. That could change a lot of things.

The good thing is that whichever way it goes, you will be happier with your life. That's the whole purpose of tidying up—that is, so you will be happier. After all, there is no award that will be given out for who has the tidiest house, but being a happy person is its own reward.

Bottom line: Once your house is tidy, give life some time and be open-minded. Some things may change. Whether they do or not, you will be a much happier person.

One of the best things to come out of tidying up your house is that you now know how to make decisions (and take actions) on what inspires joy in your life.

Chapter 8

Your Happy Dance Begins with Your House and Life in Order

"Think of how stupid the average person is, and realize half of them are stupider than that."

~ *George Calin*

Your house is in order, but before you start your happy dance make sure your life is in order if you want to really experience joy. Just because you now have a tidy house doesn't necessarily mean that your life is tidy and in order. And without your house <u>and</u> your life in order, you can't have the happy, stress-free lifestyle you want.

Tidying is the first step in allowing you to achieve your true goal of having the lifestyle you want.

If you're sitting in a clean, tidy and uncluttered room and you're still having problems with anxiety, you may need to look at what's really bothering you. As long as your house is cluttered, you're not forced to look inside yourself for the true cause of your anxiety, you just think all of your stress is caused by the mess around you. Clutter keeps you from looking at what's really bothering you.

Now that you've gotten rid of the clutter, you can get rid of the other problems too.

Here's the next step.

Declare a Statute of Limitations

We can learn from the past and from our mistakes, but you can declare a statute of limitations on how long you're required to keep regret and guilt in your life. These things may serve a purpose for a short period of time, but you don't have to store them forever.

Take all of the grief, guilt, and regret in your life and throw it in the trash along with the other things that don't inspire joy in your life. You may have been storing these things for years, but now is the time to get rid of them while you're in the process of discarding things.

106

The Next Step

Once you have your house tidy and before you start buying more stuff and bringing it home, ask yourself why you placed so much value on having stuff in the first place. You know that stuff doesn't make you happy. If it did, you would already be on top of the world because heaven only knows, you had enough stuff.

Think about all of that stuff you've just thrown away or given away. Wouldn't you like to have the full retail price of what you paid for all of that stuff you have discarded?

Stop Buying So Much Stuff

Here are the techniques that will help you stay on the wagon and kick the habit of buying stuff.

- Embrace the fact that going shopping should no longer be a form of entertainment.

- Don't buy on impulse. Wait at least a week and see if you still want the item.

- Buy things online (Amazon, eBay, etc.). Don't go into stores and then get tempted to buy other things you had not intended to buy (and don't want or need).

- Think about what you're going to discard when you bring something new into the house.

When these actions become a habit, you will no longer be

dragging bags of stuff into the house every week. Problem solved.

Most people buy things for the same reason they eat—to satisfy a craving. Change your thinking. You can't have a tidy house if you're constantly buying things you don't need or even want.

Make sure that what Will Rogers said in the quote below doesn't describe you.

"Too many people spend money they haven't earned to buy things they don't want to impress people they don't like."

~ Will Rogers

Bottom line: Now you can start your happy dance.

Summary

"A house is just a place to keep your stuff while you go out and get more stuff."

~ George Carlin

After reading this far, you're armed with the knowledge and skills to tidy up your house in a way that will work. But the most important thing is that you're motivated to make it happen. You know that all of the conventional techniques you've tried in the past won't work.

I think you knew this before you read this book because you have tried all of them at one time or another and your house still isn't even close to being tidy.

The process of Tidying up is not a fun task. You just want to get it done, so don't drag it out. Do it as quickly as possible and get on with enjoying your tidy house, life and world.

Once you have your house tidy, it will never revert to a disorganized mess again because you will have made tidying a regular habit. Tidying is a mind-set and after you've done the things described in this book you will have developed that mind-set.

Tidying is a once-in-a-lifetime chore. After that one-time event, the only other tidying you will ever need to do is to once a month go through your stuff and throw more stuff away. Stuff will accumulate. Some people only do this every three months because they say that not much stuff accumulates in just one month. Of course, if you threw something away every time you bought something new, you might only have to do this every six months.

(By the way, picking up things and putting them back in their place is not tidying. I call that maintenance.)

Now you can actually say that your lifestyle brings you joy.

How your house looks after you've finished tidying is the easiest change to see, but the greatest change will likely be what you can't see. You'll start liking yourself and you'll gain a lot of confidence. This will change how other people see you, doors will open, life will be fun and exciting, and you will start to really enjoy your life.

I don't mean that you're going to immediately find wealth or the love of your life (of course, you might find both), but you will almost immediately learn to like yourself and your life. The confidence you will gain will change a lot of things for you. People like to be around confident people. The new friends you will attract will likely be fun-loving, achievers, positive thinkers, and interesting souls. Enjoy their company and your new life. I think it's safe to say that after you finish tidying up you will experience a transformation in your life. You will be a new you.

Now that you know how to tidy up your house, don't forget to also tidy up your car and your space at work. You will experience the same joy when the process is completed. When tidying up your car and your space at work, you will experience a whole lot of joy for very little work.

Remember that tidying up doesn't just mean getting rid of clutter. The real reason for tidying up is to find the things that bring joy to your life, get them out where you can see them and use them so you can live and enjoy a happy life. This can't happen until you've gone through the tidying up process.

After you've read this book and implemented the techniques I've described, you can truly say that you've experienced (as the subtitle of the book says)... **The Magic and Secrets of Decluttering Your Home and Your Life**

When you get your house in order and experience the magic of an organized, clutter-free, tidy house, you may find yourself singing the song from the Disney movie *Song of the South*. It goes like this:

Zip-A-Dee-Doo-Dah

Zip-A-Dee-A

My oh my, what a wonderful day

Plenty of sunshine heading my way

Zip-A-Dee-Doo-Dah

Zip-A-Dee-A

If you have questions for me, feel free to email me at Jminchey@gmail.com.

If you found this book useful, please go to Amazon and leave a review.

Reviews are greatly appreciated.

Other Books by the Author

(You can find these books on Amazon.)

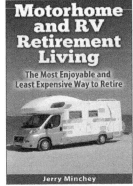

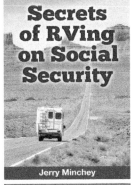

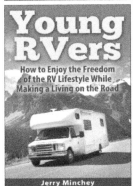

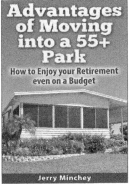

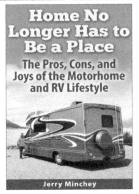

About the Author

Jerry Minchey is an engineer, author, and business manager. He has a Bachelor's degree in Electrical Engineering, an MBA from USC, and an OPM degree from Harvard Business School. He worked for NASA on the Apollo moon mission and worked for many years as a computer design engineer. He has five patents and a private pilot's license with an instrument rating. He also enjoys playing old time mountain fiddle music.

He has owned several engineering and marketing businesses. He is semi-retired now and is the founder and editor of three Internet subscription websites:

- LifeRV.com

- MarketingYourRestaurant.com

- SearchEngineU.com

As an engineer and a business manager, he looks at problems from a logical standpoint as well as an economical and financial standpoint. He has written 11 books following this format of analysis and presentation.

That's the approach he took when he analyzed and tested the tidying techniques to find out what works and what doesn't.

He lives full time in his 34 ft. Class A motorhome and spends the summer months in the North Carolina Mountains and the winter months at the Florida beaches. He also makes several side trips throughout the year to music festivals, workshops, and to a rally or two when he finds one he likes. He says, "Home is wherever I park it."

####

Made in United States
Orlando, FL
23 January 2022

13946126R00068